WELCOME

There's no one in the world quite like Harry Styles. This singer, songwriter, fashion innovator and rising star actor has carved out a stratospheric career in just over a decade. From tending to a bakery and competing in local battle of the bands competitions in his early days to winning success with One Direction in The X Factor and now taking over the world as a solo artist and winning three Grammys, Harry's rise to the top has been epic and well-deserved. In this special activity book, we pay tribute to the magnetic superstar with a series of illustrations you can colour to how you see fit. That's not all, though: there are wordsearches, quizzes and other activities perfect for any superfan. Get ready to enter the wild world of Harry…

FUTURE

FUTURE

HARRY STYLES
COLOURING & ACTIVITY BOOK

Future PLC Quay House, The Ambury, Bath, BA1 1UA

Harry Styles Colouring & Activity Book Editorial
Editor **Drew Sleep**
Designer **Harriet Knight**
Illustrator **Kym Winters**
Compiled by **Dan Peel & Harriet Knight**
Senior Art Editor **Andy Downes**
Head of Art & Design **Greg Whitaker**
Editorial Director **Jon White**
Managing Director **Grainne McKenna**

Images
Getty Images
All copyrights and trademarks are recognised and respected

Advertising
Media packs are available on request
Commercial Director **Clare Dove**

International
Head of Print Licensing **Rachel Shaw**
licensing@futurenet.com
www.futurecontenthub.com

Circulation
Head of Newstrade **Tim Mathers**

Production
Head of Production **Mark Constance**
Production Project Manager **Matthew Eglinton**
Advertising Production Manager **Joanne Crosby**
Digital Editions Controller **Jason Hudson**
Production Managers **Keely Miller, Nola Cokely, Vivienne Calvert, Fran Twentyman**

Printed in the UK

Distributed by Marketforce, 5 Churchill Place, Canary Wharf, London, E14 5HU
www.marketforce.co.uk – For enquiries, please email:
mfcommunications@futurenet.com

Harry Styles Colouring & Activity Book Third Edition (CTB5566)
© 2023 Future Publishing Limited

We are committed to only using magazine paper which is derived from responsibly managed, certified forestry and chlorine-free manufacture. The paper in this bookazine was sourced and produced from sustainable managed forests, conforming to strict environmental and socioeconomic standards.

All contents © 2023 Future Publishing Limited or published under licence. All rights reserved. No part of this magazine may be used, stored, transmitted or reproduced in any way without the prior written permission of the publisher. Future Publishing Limited (company number 2008885) is registered in England and Wales. Registered office: Quay House, The Ambury, Bath BA1 1UA. All information contained in this publication is for information only and is, as far as we are aware, correct at the time of going to press. Future cannot accept any responsibility for errors or inaccuracies in such information. You are advised to contact manufacturers and retailers directly with regard to the price of products/services referred to in this publication. Apps and websites mentioned in this publication are not under our control. We are not responsible for their contents or any other changes or updates to them. This magazine is fully independent and not affiliated in any way with the companies mentioned herein.

Future plc is a public company quoted on the London Stock Exchange (symbol: FUTR)
www.futureplc.com

Chief Executive Officer **Jon Steinberg**
Non-Executive Chairman **Richard Huntingford**
Chief Financial and Strategy Officer **Penny Ladkin-Brand**

Tel +44 (0)1225 442 244

Colouring

THE X FACTOR

A young Harry entered the seventh series of the UK talent show *The X Factor* in 2010. He first competed as a solo artist but shifted gears and became part of the group One Direction.

Colouring

OVERNIGHT FAME

After their third-place finish in the *X Factor* final, One Direction became instant superstars. They immediately signed to Simon Cowell's record label and jetted off to the US to write their first album.

Colouring

HATS OFF!

Each 1D member got involved with the songwriting process as their careers progressed. Liam and Louis wrote the most, while Harry still had a hand in many of the group's hits.

Colouring

BUTTERFLY

Harry has a giant butterfly inked across his stomach. This could represent transformation, marking Harry's shifting career from 1D band member to a solo artist, fashionista and even actor.

Colouring

CENTRE STAGE

Harry's energetic stage presence has drawn comparisons with some of the most legendary performers in music, such as Queen's Freddie Mercury and The Rolling Stones' Mick Jagger.

ANCHOR

Harry's anchor tattoo on his lower left arm is actually a cover-up of a previous tattoo. The original spelled the words "I can't change" across the singer's wrist... well, maybe he changed his mind.

Colouring

MAN OF THE MATCH

Harry is not afraid to show off his sporty side. In 2014, he took part in Niall Horan's Charity Football Challenge with his 1D band-mates Liam Payne and Louis Tomlinson.

Colouring

HAIR-RAISER

He might have settled into a more regular hairstyle in his late 20s, but Harry spent a lot of time experimenting with his hair early in his career. At its longest, it looked like a lion's mane!

Colouring

ROSES

A rose is the calling card for the greatest emotion: love. Harry is a romantic and has dated many high-profile names across his life, including Taylor Swift, Kendall Jenner and Olivia Wilde.

Colouring

TALK OF THE TOWN

Pop stars aren't strangers to the talk show circuit, and Harry Styles enjoys showing off his charismatic personality with regular appearances on the likes of James Corden's *Late Late Show*.

Colouring

FERN

Harry must be a lover of plants as he has two ferns tatooed across his lower abdomen. These leafy flora tats cover up another tattoo that Harry perhaps felt he outgrew that said "might as well".

26

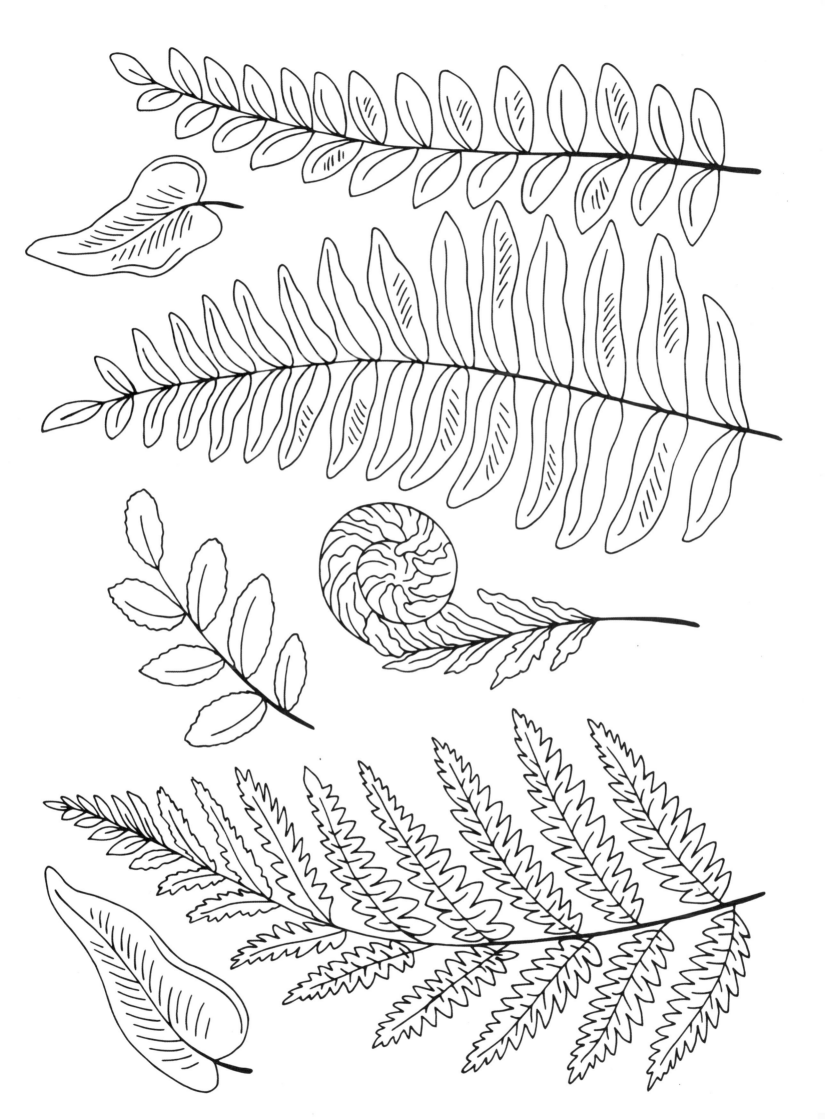

Colouring

HARRY THE HOST

He might be a confident guest on TV talk shows, but Harry is also a magnetic frontman behind the desk. He's sat in for James Corden and hosted the comedy hit Saturday Night Live.

Colouring

TIGER

Tigers are noble creatures so it's no surprise that Harry chose to decorate a thigh with a homage to this beautiful animal. One of Harry's former 1D band-mates, Zayn, also has a tattoo of a tiger.

Colouring

HARRY X ELTON

Harry's glam approach to his on-stage presence harks back to Elton John. For Halloween 2018, Harry paid tribute to the music legend by recreating this iconic 1975 baseball outfit.

Colouring

FASHION ICON

Harry has always had a careful eye for fashion, and when he co-chaired the Met Gala fashion show in 2019, all eyes were on him. His gender-fluid gown and earrings were breathtaking.

Colouring

SWALLOW

Back in olden times, sailors would get tattoos of these birds to represent their sailing experience. Harry's swallows symbolise how much he has travelled across his career.

Colouring

BOOGIE DOWN

Harry's on-stage outfits never disappoint. For this performance in New York City, he channelled 1970s chic with high-waisted flares and a gender-neutral pink Gucci blazer.

38

Colouring

MERMAID

When Harry was asked by Hollywoodlife.com about the inspiration behind his mermaid tattoo, located next to the anchor on his left arm, he cheekily replied, "I am a mermaid."

40

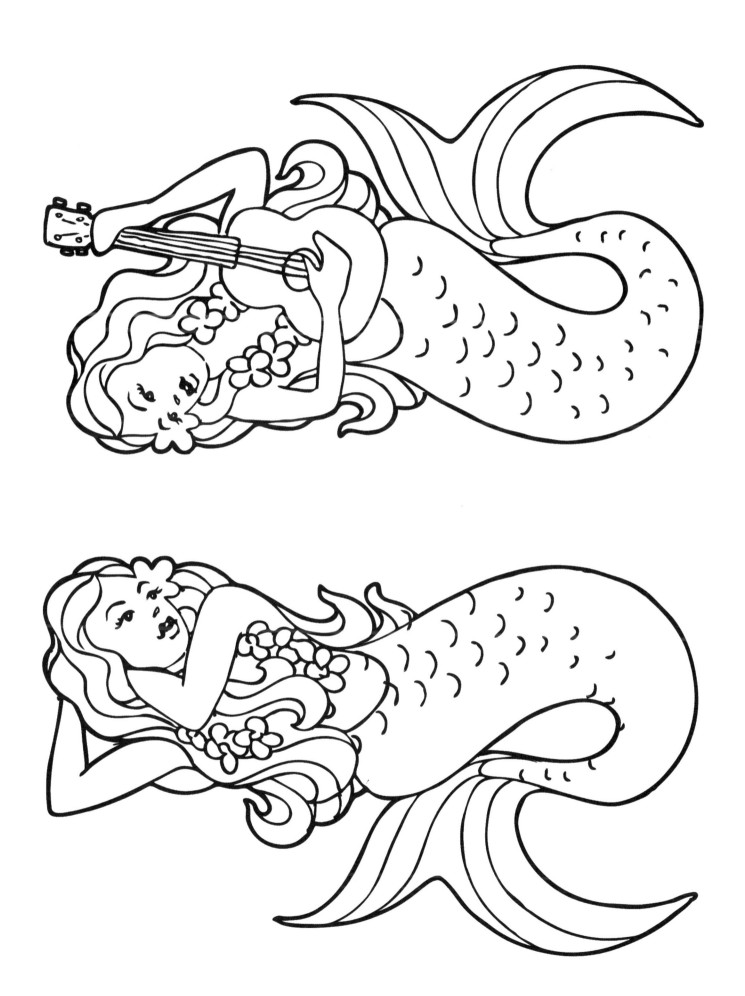

Colouring

SUIT UP

Recently, Harry has fully leaned into his love for the jumpsuit. Whether it's a music video or a live show, if Harry is singing, you can expect him to be performing in one of these colourful ensembles.

Colouring

CLOWN AROUND

Harry's music video for his song 'Daylight' was recorded in three hours. Harry and his pal James Corden knocked on random New York City apartment doors to find a place to shoot in.

44

Colouring

MUSIC

Harry's musical ability has grown from strength to strength. From mastering his voice to instruments like the guitar and piano, and proving himself a capable songwriter, Harry is a master of the art.

46

Colouring

IN FULL FEATHER

Harry's recent love affair with the feathered boa has captured the eyes of the fashion world. He often uses one to add flair to some of his more conventional looks, like this leather jacket.

Colouring

HOUSE OF HARRY

For the launch of Harry's second album *Fine Line*, Spotify created a listening experience for fans, complete with themed murals. Harry himself put in an appearance, thanking his fans.

50

Colouring

Festival fanatic

Coachella in California, USA, is one of the world's most popular festivals, and artists are expected to bring their A-game. Harry stunned watchers in his 2022 performance, thanks to this bombastic outfit.

Colouring

TOP OF HIS GAME

2022 has been a new golden age for Harrymania. He has released an acclaimed new album, *Harry's House*, experimented with his on and off-stage style, and won more starring acting roles.

Colouring

WATERMELON

Reaching the top ten charts of more than 20 countries, Harry Styles' song 'Watermelon Sugar' has been a roaring success. The catchy tune has topped well over a billion streams on Spotify.

Colouring

SHINE ON

Harry first found his love for performing music when his band White Eskimo won a 'battle of the bands' competition. "I think I was just a show-off," he told *Rolling Stone*. "I say that like it's past tense."

Colouring

EAR FOR QUALITY

Harry grew up listening to the likes of The Beatles, The Rolling Stones and Fleetwood Mac, and he points to those bands as influences in his own music along with Shania Twain.

Colouring

EAGLE

These powerful hunters of the sky are a popular choice of tattoo. Harry's eagle acts as another cover-up for a previous ink on his right forearm that said "things I can".

Colouring

MOON MAN

In October 2021 Harry hosted 'Harryween' a concert with a Halloween twist. He donned several cool costumes, including this fascinating lunar-themed outfit.

Colouring

HEADLINE HARRY

Harry closed the BBC's Big Weekend 2022 with a powerful setlist of tracks. He wowed the audience with new hits like 'As It Was' and even brought out a 1D classic: 'What Makes You Beautiful'.

Colouring

FAN FAVOURITE

Harry has lived in the spotlight for over a decade and has a super-strong fanbase. Like many artists, Harry has a good relationship with his fans, taking the time to interact with them when he can.

68

Colouring

ACT THE PART

Harry's acting career began when he was cast in Christopher Nolan's *Dunkirk*. Since then, he's played Eros in Marvel's *Eternals* and is set to have a starring role in *My Policeman*.

Colouring

SHIP

Old-timey ships make for pretty cool tattoos, especially when you consider that Harry Styles has one on his upper left arm. Harry has said it reminds him of travelling home while on tour.

Colouring

DRESS FOR SUCCESS

Harry's approach to the clothes he wears is fluid. Put simply: he wears whatever he wants to. "What's exciting about right now is you can wear what you like," he told *Variety*.

Colouring

BIRDCAGE

On Harry's upper-left torso is a tattoo of an empty birdcage. This ink was one of Harry's earliest tattoos and was first spotted in 2012. No one but Harry really knows what it symbolises.

76

Colouring

ALBUM OF THE YEAR

In August 2022, *Harry's House* won Album of the Year at MTV's VMA awards. "I know this is a fan-voted award [...] I wouldn't be holding this if it wasn't for you," Harry said in his speech.

78

ON SALE NOW!

The perfect gift for any Harry Styles fan

From One Direction to solo superstardom, and from Holmes Chapel to Hollywood, over the past decade Harry Styles has become a global sensation. This special edition celebrates every step of his phenomenal career so far.

Ordering is easy. Go online at:

WWW.MAGAZINESDIRECT.COM

Or get it from selected supermarkets & newsagents

ACTIVITIES

82 Labyrinth
83 Design a jumpsuit

WORDSEARCHES
84 Tattoos
86 Songs
88 Fashion

QUIZZES
90 Easy
92 Medium
94 Hard

96 Answers

Tattoos

```
O T E A H W I S T A R A S W
T L L R C M E R M A I D E S
F E G A C D R I B E C R W E
B A S T R H A R F C A O A S
U P R H T B S A B E L E A F
T T N L F D R E J L C D S L
T C R O S S H E A A E D I E
E O G E C O E W R R W Y T L
R H D H A D S R E R V O A H
F F W H A N D S H A K E D E
L A R B W F D R D R E T T A
Y T S K E L E T O N O A E R
D K M G F P U O M E L J A T
R A N C H O R R S T R H S E
```

FIND THESE WORDS...

ANCHOR   CROSS   MERMAID   SWALLOWS
BIRDCAGE   HANDSHAKE   SKELETON
BUTTERFLY   HEART   STAR

Wordsearch

WORDSEARCH
Songs

FIND THESE WORDS...

ADOREYOU	GOLDEN	SIGNOFTHETIMES
ASITWAS	KIWI	TPWK
FALLING	LIGHTSUP	TWOGHOSTS
		WATERMELON

WORDSEARCH
Fashion

```
R E Z A L B I L P H M I S A
J S R O S V L K B A W K E P
O R F I K N H O N H P A Q F
D U O T I D V H U J E M U I
H P C R N E O C W S Q P I D
U W B O N B J T L K E Z N K
N C N T I L I D L G U C S O
S S F R E U W V L H P W C G
G F Z P S P A U S N E M F J
E K U P B A Q N M A B R Q T
N S M I U B L H T S A L E I
G U T R E L G E L C O S B F
J A X P E A R L S O W I D M
L B E R S S F N H S T O O B
```

FIND THESE WORDS...

BOOTS BLAZER PURSE SEQUINS
       BLOUSE JUMPSUIT SKINNIES
       PEARLS SCARF SWEATER

Fashion

Quizzes

HOW WELL DO YOU KNOW HARRY?
EASY

1 What was the name of Harry's band before he went solo?

.. ..

2 Which country in the British Isles is Harry from?
- ☐ ENGLAND
- ☐ SCOTLAND
- ☐ WALES
- ☐ NORTHERN IRELAND
- ☐ IRELAND

3 Unscramble this anagram into a hit Harry solo single:

LAWMEN OUTRAGERS

.. ..

Hint: Sweet treat

4 What was the name of the TV singing competition that Harry auditioned for at the start of his career in 2010?

.. ..

5 What does Harry's motto TPWK stand for?
- ☐ TALL PEOPLE WALK KITTENS
- ☐ THE PEOPLE WILL KNEEL
- ☐ TREAT PEOPLE WITH KINDNESS
- ☐ TO PAY WITH KISSES

6 Harry is also an actor.
☐ TRUE or ☐ FALSE

7 Which one of these singers WASN'T a member of Harry's band?
- ☐ LOUIS TOMLINSON
- ☐ ZAYN MALIK
- ☐ LIAM PAYNE
- ☐ SHAWN MENDES
- ☐ NIALL HORAN

8 What line follows:

IN THIS WORLD, IT'S JUST US

in the chorus of the track

AS IT WAS?

.. ..

9 Which of these solo albums came first?
- ☐ HARRY'S HOUSE
- ☐ HARRY STYLES
- ☐ FINE LINE

10 What colour eyes does Harry have?

.. ..

Quizzes

HOW WELL DO YOU KNOW HARRY?
MEDIUM

1 What job did Harry work as before becoming a singer?

....

2 In what film did Harry make his cinematic debut?

....

3 Harry auditioned to play the role of David Bowie, but the director thought he was too famous to take on the role.

☐ TRUE or ☐ FALSE

4 Which song is Harry's most-streamed song on Spotify? (As of September 2022)

☐ ADORE YOU
☐ AS IT WAS
☐ WATERMELON SUGAR
☐ SIGN OF THE TIMES

5 Complete the lyric:
WE NEVER LEARN, WE'VE BEEN HERE BEFORE...

....
....

6 Unscramble this song title:
ANGLE HALT KITTING

....
Hint: Not getting any sleep tonight

7 What year did Harry launch his solo career by releasing his first single, Sign Of The Times?

....

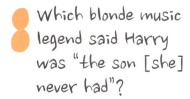

8 Which blonde music legend said Harry was "the son [she] never had"?

☐ COURTNEY LOVE
☐ DEBBIE HARRY
☐ DOLLY PARTON
☐ STEVIE NICKS

9 What is Harry's Twitter handle?

☐ @H_SWIZ
☐ @TPWK
☐ @HARRY_STYLES
☐ @STYLES

10 Harry was the first solo male to appear on the cover of Vogue magazine?

☐ TRUE or ☐ FALSE

Quizzes

HOW WELL DO YOU KNOW HARRY?
HARD

1 Which of these songs did Harry sing for his first X Factor audition?

- ☐ ISN'T SHE LOVELY? – STEVIE WONDER
- ☐ ASTRAL WEEKS – VAN MORRISON
- ☐ FLY ME TO THE MOON – FRANK SINATRA
- ☐ HEY THERE DELILAH – PLAIN WHITE T'S

2 Harry's 2019 Met Gala outfit drew eyes and won him a lot of media coverage. What did he wear?

- ☐ A SEE-THROUGH BLACK GUCCI BLOUSE
- ☐ A WHITE PRADA DRESS EMBROIDERED WITH MESSAGES FROM FANS
- ☐ A COCO CHANEL CABARET COSTUME
- ☐ HIS CHILDHOOD PYJAMAS, REMADE BY LADY GAGA'S HAUS OF GAGA

3 In which city was Harry Styles born?

....

4 Harry has a role in Marvel's Cinematic Universe, but as who?

....

5 What was the name of Harry's band before One Direction?

....

6 What Harry Styles song is inspired by a classic childhood book by Roald Dahl?

....

94

Hard

7 Unscramble this song title:

FASHIONSAMURAI STRUCTURES

.. ..

Hint: A nice meal out…

8 What day is Harry's birthday?

.. ..

9 Who directed the film 'Don't Worry Darling', starring Harry and Florence Pugh?

.. ..

10 What is Harry's middle name?

.. ..

ANSWERS

LABYRINTH

SONGS

WORDSEARCHES
TATTOOS

FASHION

Answers

HOW WELL DO YOU KNOW HARRY?

EASY

1. One Direction
2. England
3. Watermelon Sugar
4. The X Factor
5. Treat People With Kindness
6. True
7. Shawn Mendes
8. You know it's not the same as it was
9. Harry Styles
10. Green

MEDIUM

1. A baker (at the W Manderville Bakery, if you're a real superfan!)
2. Dunkirk
3. False. He auditioned for the title role of Baz Luhrmann's Elvis
4. Watermelon Sugar
5. Why are we always stuck and running from the bullets?
6. Late Night Talking
7. 2017
8. Stevie Nicks
9. Harry_Styles
10. True

HARD

1. Isn't She Lovely - Stevie Wonder
2. A Black Gucci Blouse
3. Redditch
4. Eros/Starfox
5. White Eskimo
6. Matilda
7. Music For A Sushi Restaurant
8. 1 February
9. Olivia Wilde
10. Edward